Coke Goes to War

by V. Dennis Wrynn

Pictorial Histories Publishing Co.
Missoula, Montana

Library of Congress Catalog Card No. 96-68231
ISBN 1-57510-016-9

First Printing: May, 1996

Pictorial Histories Publishing Co., Inc.
713 South Third Street
Missoula, Montana 59801

CONTENTS

ACKNOWLEDGMENTS

DURING THE FIRST HALF of this century national magazines were the major advertising vehicle for most of the nation's large companies. The Coca-Cola Company has been an advertising leader throughout its long history, and the World War II years were no exception. While many corporations strained credulity while attempting to identify their products with the war effort, Coke had no difficulty in this area as the advertisements featured in this book will attest. The famous soft drink was already an integral part of most American lives, and its reputation grew stronger as a result of its wartime popularity.

I wish to thank CocaCola USA for giving me permission to publish these impressive advertisements. I also owe a special thanks to Ms. Pam Weldon, owner of Liberty Park Antiques in Fredericksburg, Virginia. Her generous assistance and the availability of her personal Coca-Cola memorabilia collection were invaluable in the preparation of this book. My appreciation also to Marty Coburn, owner of Collectvs Books in Fredericksburg, and to WWII naval veteran John Gecan of Falls Church, Virginia, both of whom were also of assistance on this project.

V. DENNIS WRYNN
Fairfax Station, Virginia
December, 1995

INTRODUCTION

DURING THE SECOND WORLD WAR 15 million men and women were members of the American armed services. They were stationed all over the globe, in exciting and exotic locales as well as places that were dull and boring. And many of these young Americans were engaged in deadly combat with experienced and powerful enemy forces.

Much of the world had been at war for several years before the Japanese surprise attack at Pearl Harbor in December 1941 brought the United States into the conflict. Military and civilian casualties already numbered in the millions, and the war would go on another three years and nine months. Although the American people were shocked by Japanese successes in the early months of 1942 that included the capture of Guam and Wake Island and the fall of the Philippines, they were heartened by the Doolittle air raid on Tokyo in April 1942 followed by the US Navy's victory at the Battle of Midway in June. The United States had started the long road back.

The youthful Americans who fill the ranks of their country's military organizations were enthusiastic exporters of the nation's culture, and often overwhelmed their host nations with their attitudes, music, cigarettes, food and, universally, Coca-Cola.

By the beginning of WWII, Coca-Cola was already 55 years old and was far ahead of its competitors in sales, as well as in advertising and marketing. It was also international in scope, with distribution of its soda fountain syrup solidly in place before 1920. France was the location of the first overseas bottling plant in 1926, and two years later Coke was available at the Olympic Games in Amsterdam. It was also prominent at the Berlin Olympics in 1936 (Berlin was the site of a modern Coca-Cola bottling plant) and was the first company to receive a display contract for the New York World's Fair in 1939. The exhibit included a model bottling plant and offered a color movie entitled *Refreshment Through the Years.*

By 1941 Coca-Cola was bottled in 44 countries. After America's entry into the war, the company's chairman, Robert Woodruff, pledged to make Coca-Cola available to servicemen and women anywhere in the world without increasing the 5 cents per bottle price maintained at home. During the next four years 64 Coca-Cola bottling plants were constructed on foreign soil to provide America's favorite soft drink to her sons and daughters abroad. Nearly 250 company employees were given quasi-military status as T.O.s, technical observers, and followed the troops to every continent barring Antarctica, providing Coca-Cola to the boys and girls in the service. These T.O.s wore Army uniforms and were given officer's rank. Two were killed during the war. Most were involved in building or converting existing bottling plants in far off places, with enemy prisoners of war often used as willing workers. As a result, more than five billion bottles of Coke, plus uncounted soda fountain drinks, were imbibed by service personnel and the local inhabitants of countries where the US soldiers, sailors and airmen were stationed.

At home Coca-Cola continued its highly visible and sophisticated advertising campaigns, several of which were developed in conjunction with military themes and national attitudes. The soft drink's scripted name and red trademark were and had been for many years instantly recognizable, a status sought by many companies but attained by very few. Coke was to soft drinks what Kleenex was to tissues; a brand name that became synonymous with the product.

This book chronicles Coca-Cola's unrivaled national magazine advertisements during the years of the Second World War. From 1907 until 1955 the company's advertising agency was D'Arcy Advertising headed by William D'Arcy. Although located in St. Louis, the agency opened a New York office in 1935 at Coca-Cola's request. Illustrators employed in the production of Coca-Cola magazine ads included Norman Rockwell and Haddon Sundblom. The human subjects were universally attractive and healthy, and the ads often featured as their central themes the social interaction between young men and women as well as interesting and exciting locations. Most important was the local soda fountain.

By the early spring of 1942 Coke had injected Home Front defense production into its magazine ads, and by the summer months US soldiers in training for combat were being portrayed. These advertisements were followed later in the year by the "That Extra Something! - you can spot it every time" campaign depicting different aspects of American servicemen's duty stations and respon-sibilities around the world and the nation as well as civilians doing their duty at home. Interspersed in these ads were the familiar slogans associated with Coke - "the taste of quality", "pause - be refreshed". The "Extra Something" series was phased out in mid-1943 and the new theme expressed was COKE = FRIENDSHIP (in one form or another). Often the ads illustrated the introduction of both Coca-Cola and American servicemen to their native hosts and featured the foreign country's language. This campaign theme was retained by Coca-Cola throughout the rest of the war, and was often referred to as the global high-sign. However, the company would never totally identify with only one advertising campaign. It often re-utilized successful slogans and advertisements from previous strategies. One old slogan was modified during the war, becoming "the pause that refreshes", and it remained in use for many years after WWII had ended.

There is no doubt that Coca-Cola's popularity was genuine during the Second World War, and there is also no doubt that its availability all over the wartime world contributed to its tremendous growth after hostilities had ended. Other soft drink companies could grouse, but it was clearly obvious that Coke was the soft drink of choice for millions of servicemen and women. Coca-Cola continues today as the world's leading non-alcoholic libation, and its advertising campaigns, which of course have changed with the times, continue to set standards for other to emulate and envy.

Drink
Coca-Cola
Delicious and Refreshing

ICE-COLD EVERY DAY IN THE YEAR
5¢

COCA-COLA CO., ATLANTA, GA

Thru 50 years...1886 to 1936
The pause that refreshes

Fashions in clothes change. But human thirst is always the same. Since the first ice-cold Coca-Cola made a *pause refreshing* in 1886, its fame has spread . . . from city to city . . . country to country . . . around the world . . . welcome everywhere, because ice-cold Coca-Cola is what refreshment ought to be . . . pure . . . wholesome . . . delicious.

Although the United States was in the midst of an economic depression in 1936, the world was at peace and Coca-Cola was 50 years old. The company celebrated its anniversary in this advertisement by highlighting the change in womens' bathing attire—from middie blouse to a revealing, abbreviated one-piece swim suit. The swimmers' shoes, however, remained remarkably the same from one generation to another, as are the Cokes the ladies are drinking. (1936)

Pause and refresh

Drink Coca-Cola

Delicious and Refreshing

A good place to park...and to pause...is where you see the familiar red sign that says "Drink Coca-Cola." On streets and highways everywhere it flashes a welcome invitation to a sociable pause for pure refreshment. Thirst asks nothing more.

"COLD...ICE-COLD"

In 1938, the national economy was improving, and these three young ladies are able to enjoy a trip in a convertible to the local drive-in restaurant for a Coke. Automobile front seats were somewhat wider in those days. (1938)

The theme of the New York World's Fair in 1939 was "the World of Tomorrow", and Coca-Cola was the first company to receive a display contract for this fabulous international fair—the last before WWII brought such visionary endeavors to an abrupt halt. The exhibit featured a model bottling plant and offered a color movie about Coke entitled *Refreshment Through The Years*. On the opposite coast, San Francisco celebrated "the Pageant of the Pacific", which hopefully was not a foretaste of the carnage that would envelop the Pacific a few years later. (1939)

Thirst stops here

The road maps of the world are dotted with happy places to pause. And ice-cold Coca-Cola is there to make a pause *the pause that refreshes*. Familiar red coolers everywhere signal you to refresh yourself and be off to a fresh start.

COPYRIGHT 1939, THE COCA-COLA COMPANY

DRINK Coca-Cola

INVITING YOU TO PAUSE...REFRESH

By the late 1930s many Coca-Cola coolers were refrigerated electrically. However, those on the outside porch of the local gas station where they were exposed to the weather, as well as the driver's eye, still used block ice. (1939)

Drink **Coca-Cola**
Delicious and Refreshing

The pause that refreshes
...at home

COPYRIGHT 1939, THE COCA-COLA COMPANY

Housework brings that urge to pause and relax in an easy chair. Do it...with ice-cold Coca-Cola. It adds to relaxation what relaxation always needs ...pure, wholesome refreshment.

REFRESH YOURSELF WITH ICE-COLD COCA-COLA ... FROM YOUR OWN REFRIGERATOR

Coke's magazine advertisements during 1939 revived the phrase *the pause that refreshes*, which was first introduced in a *Saturday Evening Post* ad in 1929. This young woman, with her modern upright vacuum cleaner beside her, takes a break from her household chores. (1939)

It's a lucky thirst that meets an ice-cold Coca-Cola...at America's favorite meeting place, the soda fountain. Coca-Cola has the taste thirst goes for. It leaves you with an after-sense of complete refreshment ...making a pause *the pause that refreshes.*

The soda fountain was a popular meeting place in the 1930s and 40s. This attractive young couple are nattily attired for summer, including straw hats and, in the man's case, a white linen suit. The tray advertisement at the top of the photo insert features another popular Coke advertising slogan, *Thirst Stops Here.* (1939)

A whole gamut of healthy, involved people were featured in this end of year magazine advertisement, including an American Indian, commercial airline crew members, a young shopper and several happy baseball players. "Whoever you are, whatever you do . . ." The only one not having a Coke is the snow-shoveler, as he has his hands full. (1939)

Coca-Cola has the charm of purity. It is prepared with the finished art that comes from a lifetime of practice. Its delicious taste never loses the freshness of appeal that first delighted you...always bringing you a cool, clean sense of complete refreshment. Thirst asks nothing more.

Take off refreshed

COPYRIGHT 1940, THE COCA-COLA COMPANY

Your thirst takes wings when you treat it to ice-cold Coca-Cola. And you can find ice-cold Coca-Cola *when* and *where* you are thirsty ... for the familiar red coolers are around the corner from anywhere. Enjoy Coca-Cola ... and take off refreshed.

Drink

Coca-Cola

TRADE MARK REG. U. S. PAT. OFF.

Delicious and Refreshing

5¢

THE PAUSE THAT REFRESHES

Political sentiment in the United States was overwhelmingly isolationist in 1940, but Americans could not fully ignore the major wars then being fought in Europe and China. The pilot enjoying *the pause that refreshes* may be a military aviator, although no unit insignia adorns his flight suit and helmet. (1940)

Makes a light lunch refreshing

Coca-Cola has the charm of purity. It is prepared with the finished art that comes from a lifetime of practice. Its delicious taste never loses the freshness of appeal that first delighted you...always bringing you a cool, clean sense of complete refreshment. Thirst asks nothing more.

COPYRIGHT 1940, THE COCA-COLA COMPANY

Your favorite soda fountain, your favorite sandwich, and America's favorite refreshment ...ice-cold Coca-Cola. Quick-as-a-wink you're refreshed and on your way. That's why you hear so many busy people at lunch saying: "and a Coca-Cola." Try it yourself.

5¢

Drink
Coca-Cola
TRADE MARK REG. U. S. PAT. OFF.
Delicious and Refreshing

THE PAUSE THAT REFRESHES

This businessman was certainly well-dressed, with a three piece suit, striped tie, pin collar and snapbrim fedora. Pocket watches were very much in vogue in 1940, as were BLT sandwiches with the crust trimmed and Coca-Cola for a nickel. (1940)

Coca-Cola has the charm of purity. It is prepared with the finished art that comes from a lifetime of practice. Its delicious taste never loses the freshness of appeal that first delighted you...always bringing you a cool, clean sense of complete refreshment. Thirst asks nothing more.

Take a minute to refresh

Polishing the silver was a weekly task in pre-war American homes. Maintaining a supply of Coke in the refrigerator and taking a break from the job made the work a little easier. (1940)

COPYRIGHT 1940, THE COCA-COLA COMPANY

When you're so busy you're ready to drop ... drop into an easy chair and enjoy *the pause that refreshes* with a frosty bottle of Coca-Cola from your own refrigerator. It's a refreshing little minute that's long enough for a big rest.

Drink

Coca-Cola

TRADE MARK REG. U. S. PAT. OFF.

Delicious and Refreshing

5¢

THE PAUSE THAT REFRESHES

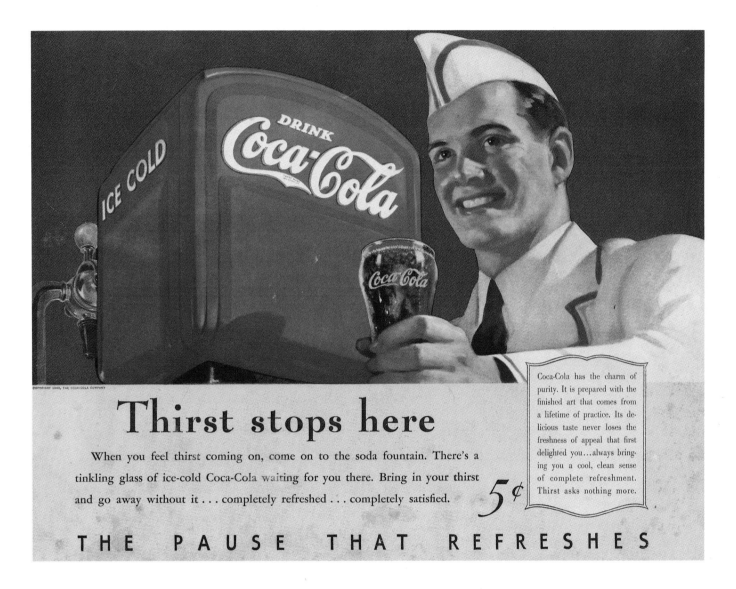

DRINK
Coca-Cola

ICE COLD

Thirst stops here

When you feel thirst coming on, come on to the soda fountain. There's a tinkling glass of ice-cold Coca-Cola waiting for you there. Bring in your thirst and go away without it . . . completely refreshed . . . completely satisfied.

5¢

Coca-Cola has the charm of purity. It is prepared with the finished art that comes from a lifetime of practice. Its delicious taste never loses the freshness of appeal that first delighted you...always bringing you a cool, clean sense of complete refreshment. Thirst asks nothing more.

THE PAUSE THAT REFRESHES

A rite of passage for many young men in small town America included a stint behind the counter as a "soda-jerk". Coca-Cola never used that derogatory appellation when describing the employees who served its product. (1940)

"Relax...take it easy"

Coca-Cola has the charm of purity. It is prepared with the finished art that comes from a lifetime of practice. Its delicious taste never loses the freshness of appeal that first delighted you...always bringing you a cool, clean sense of complete refreshment. Thirst asks nothing more.

COPYRIGHT 1940, THE COCA-COLA COMPANY

Drink
Coca-Cola
TRADE MARK REG. U.S. PAT. OFF.
Delicious and Refreshing
5¢

An easy way to take things easy is to take an ice-cold bottle of Coca-Cola...raise it to your lips...and enjoy *the pause that refreshes*. It's a refreshing short-cut to relaxation. And it's easy to do...anywhere. Enjoy an ice-cold Coca-Cola, now.

THE PAUSE THAT REFRESHES

Baseball was really the "American Game" in 1940, much more so than football or basketball, and the uniforms were flannel. Coca-Cola trucks were visible on the sidelines of many sandlot games, and Coke was being sold to the fans in major and minor league ballparks all over the country. (1940)

Coke advertising returned time and again to images of the soda fountain where it enjoyed such great success. This young lady is enjoying another of those trimmed sandwiches, and appears to be calling for her ice-cold Coca-Cola. (1940)

Thirst asks nothing more

Coca-Cola has the charm of purity. It is prepared with the finished art that comes from a lifetime of practice. Its delicious taste never loses the freshness of appeal that first delighted you...always bringing you a cool, clean sense of complete refreshment. Thirst asks nothing more.

Drink
Coca-Cola
TRADE MARK REG. U. S. PAT. OFF.
Delicious and Refreshing
5¢

Make your place in the sun a cool one. Just tip a frosty bottle of Coca-Cola to your lips. Coca-Cola, ice-cold, is cooling...so cooling. You thrill to its taste and the happy after-sense of refreshment that follows.

THE PAUSE THAT REFRESHES

When this "girl on a beach" magazine advertisement appeared in June 1940, the British Army was in the midst of its evacuation from the beaches of Dunkirk on the French coast. Germany had decisively defeated the combined Allied Armies and controlled the Continent, but the United States considered herself protected by two oceans from these ugly international conflicts. (1940)

Pause...
and shop refreshed

Coca-Cola has the charm of purity. It is prepared with the finished art that comes from a lifetime of practice. Its delicious taste never loses the freshness of appeal that first delighted you...always bringing you a cool, clean sense of complete refreshment. Thirst asks nothing more.

COPYRIGHT 1940, THE COCA-COLA COMPANY

Going from shop to shop, counter to counter, you spend something you didn't bargain on . . . energy. So when you're tired and thirsty, go straight to the soda fountain and enjoy *the pause that refreshes* with ice-cold Coca-Cola . . . a little minute that's long enough for a big rest.

Drink

Coca-Cola
TRADE MARK REG U.S. PAT. OFF.

Delicious and Refreshing

5¢

THE PAUSE THAT REFRESHES

These two attractive ladies, wearing the latest in millinery fashion, are reading the *Fashion Times* and enjoying their Coca-Colas. The advertisement was part of the "women shoppers theme" which ran through the company's 1940 promotional campaign. The economy of the United States was clearly emerging from the Depression, while war clouds were gathering all around the nation's borders. (1940)

Returning to the soda fountain theme, this wholesome young couple are about to *pause and refresh*. The woman's gloves and the man's scarf reflect the season, as this advertisement was featured in November. (1940)

Thirst knows no season

Coca-Cola has the charm of purity. It is prepared with the finished art that comes from a lifetime of practice. Its delicious taste never loses the freshness of appeal that first delighted you...always bringing you a cool, clean sense of complete refreshment. Thirst asks nothing more.

COPYRIGHT 1940, THE COCA-COLA COMPANY

Even with winter just around the corner, thirst stays on ... reminding you that around the corner from anywhere there's a soda fountain. There you'll find the warmth of summer ... companionship ... and America's "year-'round" answer to thirst...ice-cold Coca-Cola. Pause there and be refreshed.

Drink

Coca-Cola

TRADE MARK REG. U. S. PAT. OFF.

Delicious and Refreshing

5¢

THE PAUSE THAT REFRESHES

Prior to 1931, Santa Claus was artistically depicted in many different ways, quite often as an elf, and in a great variety of apparel. Artist Haddon Sundblom changed that image forever when he created a Santa Claus for Coca-Cola's advertising campaign that has become the universal Santa: rotund, cheerful and sporting a full white beard. He also was attired in a red and white suit that reflected Coca-Cola's corporate colors. Nobody has challenged the image since. (1940)

Drink **Coca-Cola** TRADE-MARK REG. U.S. PAT. OFF. Delicious and Refreshing

"Coca-Cola belongs"

It's refreshing when young folks get their heads together. What's refreshing? Ice-cold Coca-Cola, of course. What else so fittingly adds welcome refreshment to friendly companionship.

5¢

THE PAUSE THAT REFRESHES

YOU TASTE ITS QUALITY

Experience proves that nothing takes the place of quality. You taste the quality of ice-cold Coca-Cola. Again and again you enjoy the charm of its delicious taste . . . and its cool, clean after-sense of complete refreshment. Thirst asks nothing more.

COPYRIGHT 1941, THE COCA-COLA COMPANY

The phrase *Coca-Cola Belongs* subtly creates an atmosphere of the "in" crowd, and these three young ladies enjoying their Coca-Colas seem to qualify with their "All-American" good looks. It was a solid tenant of Coke's advertising that the subjects be wholesome and cheerful in appearance, and why not? (1941)

The pause for people-on-the-go

DRINK Coca-Cola

COPYRIGHT 1941. THE COCA-COLA COMPANY

People on-the-go are never too busy to go to the soda fountain. It's a place where the hurried are glad to take a minute for *the pause that refreshes* with ice-cold Coca-Cola . . . that refreshing little stop that keeps you going. Try it.

5¢

THE PAUSE THAT REFRESHES

YOU TASTE ITS QUALITY

Experience proves that nothing takes the place of quality. You taste the quality of ice-cold Coca-Cola. Again and again you enjoy the charm of its delicious taste . . . and its cool, clean after-sense of complete refreshment. Thirst asks nothing more.

In the years before television, newspapers were very effective in disseminating the news and helping to define public opinion. Reporters were often considered glamorous characters by the average citizen, and many of them had well-deserved fine reputations. This nattily-dressed representative of the "Fourth Estate" is enjoying a soda fountain Coke while awaiting his next assignment. (1941)

Thirst stops here

YOU TASTE ITS QUALITY

Experience proves that nothing takes the place of quality. You taste the quality of ice-cold Coca-Cola. Again and again you enjoy the charm of its delicious taste...and its cool, clean after-sense of complete refreshment. Thirst asks nothing more.

COPYRIGHT 1941, THE COCA-COLA COMPANY

Pause...and park your thirst at the familiar red cooler. There you'll find frosty bottles of ice-cold Coca-Cola offering you the flavor of refreshment. Stop there now and be refreshed. You'll be glad you did.

5¢

THE PAUSE THAT REFRESHES

Refreshment and recreation belong together, as this springtime magazine advertisement demonstrates. The set of golf clubs in the forefront appear to have wooden shafts. (1941)

Work
refreshed

The factory whistle became a popular symbol to Americans, warning them that it was time to go to work and of the necessity for increased industrial production in these uncertain times of international aggression by the Axis powers. Archie Lane, the advertising art director who thought of the whistle illustration for Coca-Cola, received a $1,000 pay raise on top of his normal salary increase in 1941 as a result. (1941)

The pause that refreshes

Drink **Coca-Cola**

Delicious and Refreshing

YOU TASTE ITS QUALITY

Experience proves that nothing takes the place of quality. You taste the quality of ice-cold Coca-Cola. Again and again you enjoy the charm of its delicious taste...and its cool, clean after-sense of complete refreshment. Thirst asks nothing more.

COPYRIGHT 1941, THE COCA-COLA COMPANY

There's one thing everybody will grow this month. They'll grow thirsty.

5¢ When it happens to you, that's a good time to relax and enjoy *the pause that refreshes* with a frosty bottle of ice-cold Coca-Cola. You'll like it.

War may have been in the air but so was Spring, and a lovely flower garden, along with an attractive gardener, was part of the American landscape typified in Coca-Cola's pre-war advertising. Taking a break with *the pause that refreshes* just made the moment that much better. (1941)

"Completely refreshing"

Drink Coca-Cola

There's nothing so refreshing under the sun as delicious Coca-Cola, — ice-cold and tingling with the life and sparkle of real refreshment.

It has the quality of genuine goodness. Thirst asks nothing more.

THE PAUSE THAT REFRESHES

THE TASTE THAT CHARMS AND NEVER CLOYS

You'll welcome ice-cold Coca-Cola just as often and as surely as thirst comes. You taste its quality,—the quality of genuine goodness. Ice-cold Coca-Cola gives you the taste that charms and never cloys. You get the feel of complete refreshment, buoyant refreshment. Thirst asks nothing more.

COPYRIGHT 1941, THE COCA-COLA COMPANY

A pretty girl at the beach in a demure one piece bathing suit was at the heart of the American summer experience in 1941. As military spending and industrial production increasingly brought the country out of the Depression and with employment readily available for nearly everybody, the future looked very good indeed to America's citizens. (1941)

The Coca-Cola logo in this advertisement features golden wings such as a military pilot would wear, giving just the slightest hint of the increased militarization then enveloping the nation, just two months prior to Pearl Harbor. As the ad features a man on a train, it is doubtful that the wings are meant to promote commercial airline travel! (1941)

"Thirst asks nothing more"

This happy holiday representation was published in magazines during December 1941, shortly after the Japanese attack on the United States at Pearl Harbor. Corporate advertising campaigns were planned and print-set far in advance of actual publication dates. As a result, even though war had broken out, there was very little to indicate this fact in the nation's magazine advertising. However, the golden aviator's wing are once again featured in Coke's logo. (1941)

Old Santa could tell you that the friendliest moment a busy man ever met with is *the pause that refreshes* with ice-cold Coca-Cola. So, at this busiest of seasons, of course you often hear the familiar expression "'Coca-Cola', please" or that shorter way of saying it, "I'll have a 'Coke'." Ice-cold Coca-Cola is everything your thirst could ask for.

Pause...
Go refreshed

Coca-Cola

5¢

You trust its quality

Each time you taste ice-cold Coca-Cola, you are reminded that here is the quality of genuine goodness. Experience... many a refreshing experience... has taught people everywhere to trust the quality of Coca-Cola.

COPYRIGHT 1941, THE COCA-COLA COMPANY

The youthful, elf-like creature featured in this January 1942 advertisement was known as Sprite. His creator, Haddon Sundblom, used his own facial features as his model. Although white-haired, Sprite's unlined face reflected youth and health. In the advertising copy, he refers to himself as Coke, and almost immediately the general public nicknamed him Cokie. The corporation's legal department was unhappy with this predicament, fearing trademark complications, and Sprite only appeared sporadically in Coca-Cola's advertising after the first several months of 1942. (1942)

The impact of the war on civilian life had not really taken place in the first months after Pearl Harbor, and was not yet reflected in magazine advertising. This attractive young couple are happily unaware of the sacrifices, fears and uncertainties that world war would bring to many American households. (1942)

You taste its quality

Drink
Coca-Cola
TRADE-MARK REG. U.S. PAT. OFF.
Delicious and Refreshing

I'm "Coca-Cola" known, too, as "Coke". Everybody likes to shorten words. Abbreviation is a natural law of language. You hear "Coke"...the friendly abbreviation for the trade-mark "Coca-Cola"...on every hand.

"It's the real thing"

5¢

Once you taste ice-cold "Coca-Cola", you recognize its goodness and its quality. It never fails to please . . . and to refresh. Ice-cold "Coca-Cola" brings you something original in the way of a "delicious and refreshing" drink. You'll like "Coca-Cola". . . it's *the real thing*.

COPYRIGHT 1942, THE COCA-COLA COMPANY

Civilian themes still prevailed in Coca-Cola's advertisements in April 1942.
Monogrammed dresses and blouses were a fashion symbol, but most of these disappeared
as wartime rationing restricted the clothing materials available for civilian use. (1942)

Quality
carries on

Drink
Coca-Cola
Delicious and
Refreshing

5¢

Although not specifically linked to defense production, this June 1942 advertisement featuring a masculine hand bursting through what could be a metal barrier conveys an image of strength and power not usually associated with Coca-Cola's advertising. (1942)

You work better refreshed

Very quickly the hand in the previous ad was transformed into the powerful arm of a worker in overalls, representing both the factory and the farm. America was gearing up for the most incredible industrial production in the history of mankind, and corporate patriotism rose to the occasion in its advertising. (1942)

This Army corporal doesn't appear very fatigued from his cross country hike with full pack and rifle, although most of his fellow draftees and enlistees undergoing basic training probably would not agree with his cheerful demeanor. The young men of America answered their country's call to arms by the millions, and military training began in earnest in camps all over the country. (1942)

"Howdy, friend"

DRINK
Coca-Cola
TRADE-MARK REG. U.S. PAT. OFF.

No matter where you go, somewhere near you is a big, friendly red sign with the trade-mark "Coca-Cola". It reminds you that ice-cold "Coca-Cola" is everything refreshment should be . . . a clean, exciting taste . . . quality you can trust . . . refreshment you feel. When you drink ice-cold "Coca-Cola", you know it's *the real thing*.

5¢

"I'm loyal to quality"

Refreshment is my business. Good taste is my specialty. I bring you quality appeal . . . goodness that keeps on being good. I'm "Coca-Cola", known, too, as "Coke". Ice-cold "Coca-Cola" is always something to look forward to. Its quality carries on.

COPYRIGHT 1942, THE COCA-COLA COMPANY

The young women of America also responded to the national emergency, enlisting in the Army, Navy, Marines and Coast Guard. This advertisement features two Army nurses. The war is finally mentioned in Sprite's words in the center insert where he assures the public that "In war as in peace, I assure you quality . . ." (1942)

"Coca-Cola goes along"

Drink
Coca-Cola
TRADE MARK REG. U.S PAT. OFF.
Delicious and Refreshing

"It's the real thing"

It's natural for popular names to acquire friendly abbreviations. That's why you hear Coca-Cola called Coke. Coca-Cola and Coke mean the same thing . . . *the real thing* . . . "a single thing coming from a single source, and well known to the community".

COPYRIGHT 1942, THE COCA-COLA COMPANY

5¢

Ice-cold Coca-Cola gets a hearty welcome. It's the answer to thirst that adds refreshment. Coca-Cola has *that extra something* to do the job of complete refreshment. It has a taste that's uniquely satisfying —a quality that's unmistakable. That's why the only thing like Coca-Cola is Coca-Cola itself. Thirst asks nothing more.

Troop trains criss-crossed the United States at all hours of the day and night, carrying military personnel to camps, ports of embarkation and home on leave to visit their loved ones. In late December 1941, the president of Coca-Cola, Robert Woodruff, had announced that "We will see that every man in uniform gets a bottle of Coca-Cola for five cents, wherever he is and whatever the cost", thus endearing himself and his company's product to millions of American servicemen. (1942)

That *Extra* Something!

...You can spot it every time

Skilled workers have "know how". So have the makers of Coca-Cola. That's why you find that extra something in ice-cold Coca-Cola. Almost anybody can make a soft drink, but nobody else can make Coca-Cola.

You sense a finished art in its making which gives Coca-Cola a special quality. Its unique taste comes from a blend of pure, wholesome essences — refreshment that can't be duplicated.

What other drink of any kind could give you this special plus...this unique taste and after-sense of refreshment? When you realize that nothing takes the place of ice-cold Coca-Cola, you have millions of other folks for company. It's the best-liked soft drink on Earth — because contentment comes when you connect with a Coke.

Wartime limits the supply of Coca-Cola. Those times when you cannot get it, remember: Coca-Cola, being first choice, sells out first. Ask for it each time. No matter how short the supply, the quality of Coca-Cola will not be changed in any respect.

Simple pleasures build up morale and peace of mind. That's one reason why the enjoyment of ice-cold Coca-Cola has new meaning in wartime.

Your job at home is to relax and keep fit for tomorrow's job. Ice-cold Coca-Cola will add refreshment to your relaxation. Now that the amount of Coca-Cola is less in wartime, see that your home has a supply on hand, whenever possible. You'll be glad you did.

Long, hard-working hours tire you out.— slow up production. You need a brief rest-pause. So, when the schedule calls for time-out for a "breather", a moment for ice-cold, energy-giving Coca-Cola leads to better work.

Coca-Cola TRADE-MARK 5¢

COPYRIGHT 1942, THE COCA-COLA COMPANY

The best is always the better buy!

The fall of 1942 introduced a new Coke advertising campaign based on *That Extra Something*, featuring average Americans at work. Millions of civilians, both male and female, were involved in defense production, often relocating to states where these industries proliferated, with California being the most popular destination. Coca-Cola ads also began utilizing several photo inserts to multiply the message. (1942)

Haddon Sundblom's original model for his Coca-Cola Santa Claus was a retired salesman named Lou Prentice. When Prentice died, Sundblom used his own face for future illustrations, just as he had done for Coke's Sprite advertisements in early 1942. By December the United States had started back on the arduous road to victory over the Axis powers. Very soon casualties would begin to impact the American people. (1942)

That *Extra* Something!

...You can spot it every time

Supposing you were Old Santa Claus. What a job you'd have! Chimneys waiting everywhere . . . youngsters' gift lists to be checked. The job certainly calls for that extra something.

You'd get tired and thirsty, too. You'd want that extra something in refreshment—ice-cold Coca-Cola. Well, you'd find it in many homes everywhere. You could help yourself at the icebox and be welcome.

You'd find thirst gone and refreshment arriving. You'd thrill to the taste so delicious and distinctive that it stands alone. You'd know you were enjoying all the quality that skill and choicest ingredients could put there. You'd find refreshment going quickly into energy. You'd be ready again to shout, "Ho, Prancer! Ho, Vixen . . ."

(You can pretend you're Santa. You don't have to pretend you're enjoying an ice-cold Coca-Cola. Have one!)

It's natural for popular names to acquire friendly abbreviations. That's why you hear Coca-Cola called Coke. Coca-Cola and Coke mean the same thing . . . *the real thing* . . . "coming from a single source, and well known to the community".

When you shop, you never have to shop around for refreshment. There's always one bargain you can count on . . . a bargain in a bottle . . . ice-cold Coca-Cola. Enjoy it and shop refreshed.

Coca-Cola
TRADE-MARK
5¢

The best is always the better buy!

Happy moments at home are brighter when ice-cold Coca-Cola adds its life and sparkle. It's an old friend of the family ready to take off its cap and help out any time.

In remembering others, remember yourself. There's a package for you to open anytime . . . ice-cold Coca-Cola . . . *refreshment* all wrapped up in its own familiar bottle. Enjoy it often.

COPYRIGHT 1942, THE COCA-COLA COMPANY

That Extra Something!

...You can spot it every time

On furlough and headed home! Everybody's hometown has an extra something no other place possesses. Family ties . . . familiar things . . . familiar scenes and places. A place like the old neighborhood soda fountain, for instance. And the happy times of youth spent there.

And at the soda fountain . . . ice-cold Coca-Cola, the drink everybody remembers . . . and looks forward to. And with good reason.

Coca-Cola has always been made the quality way with quality ingredients. Coca-Cola is an original creation with a very special something to offer . . . a finished art in its making . . . a blend of wholesome flavors that creates for Coca-Cola a taste all its own. The only thing like Coca-Cola is Coca-Cola, itself. There are many things for thirst but one stands out for refreshment . . . ice-cold Coca-Cola.

The situation is always well in hand, when your hand holds a tinkling glass of ice-cold Coca-Cola. Delicious. Refreshing. No wonder "Coke-dates" are the thing.

Wartime limits the supply of Coca-Cola. Those times when you cannot get it, remember: Coke, being first choice, sells out first. Ask for it each time.

Like an occasional "leave", frequent refreshment helps morale. That's why you so often see the boys in uniform drinking ice-cold Coca-Cola.

Coca-Cola 5¢

Rigorous training on the obstacle course keeps Uncle Sam's Marines in fighting trim. After such maneuvers, they like a drink that more than quenches thirst . . . a drink of refreshing energy . . . ice-cold Coca-Cola.

The best is always the better buy!

COPYRIGHT 1942, THE COCA-COLA COMPANY

The glamour associated with a US Marine's "dress blues" induced many a young man to enlist in the Corps for the duration. The Marines landed on Guadalcanal in August 1942, and were the first American ground troops to go on the offensive as the country's war efforts went into high gear. The issue on Guadalcanal was in doubt for several months, but the gyrenes prevailed, and started the country's armed forces on the road to Tokyo. (1942)

Continuing *That Extra Something* theme, this Coca-Cola advertisement in February 1943 featured an Army private, while the photo inserts included represented members of the Navy and the Marines. By this point in the war, the Army had spearheaded the November 1942 invasion of North Africa as part of "Operation Torch". The next major battle in the Mediterranean would be the invasion of Sicily the following July. (1943)

That Extra Something!
...You can spot it every time

On the campus or off, Coca-Cola has that extra something that rates with youth. That's why Coca-Cola—a long-established product—belongs to the younger set, too, year after year. Choicest, special ingredients and special care in its making, give Coca-Cola a special refreshing taste and quality.

This unique taste comes from a finished art in its making that sets Coca-Cola apart...a blend of flavor-essences merging the ingredients of Coca-Cola into a taste all its own. And it leaves that unmistakable after-sense of refreshment that everybody recognizes ...and welcomes.

The custom in every neighborhood...to enjoy delicious ice-cold Coca-Cola at the soda fountain...though not as often in wartime as before. And remember when you sometimes can't get Coca-Cola, it's because Coke, being first choice, sells out first.

Between hard-working shifts, girls in defense jobs welcome a refreshing pause for Coke, that little minute long enough for a big rest...leading to better work.

Busy moments at home are brighter when ice-cold Coca-Cola adds its life and sparkle. It's an old friend of the family ready to take off its cap and help out any time.

It's natural for popular names to acquire friendly abbreviations. That's why you hear Coca-Cola called Coke. Both mean the same thing..."coming from a single source, and well known to the community".

Coca-Cola 5¢

The best is always the better buy!

COPYRIGHT 1943, THE COCA-COLA COMPANY

Not forgotten in this advertising campaign were the American women persevering on the Home Front. Three of the four illustrations in this ad feature student life. However, the left hand insert definitely portrays the female defense plant worker, often referred to as "Rosie the Riveter". As the war progressed and more and more men were called into military service, women played an increasingly critical role in performing work that had usually been reserved for men prior to the war. (1943)

"I'm saying this for Uncle Sam!"

FOR VICTORY

BUY
UNITED
STATES
WAR BONDS
AND
STAMPS

"I speak for the pleasant, happy things in life... all the things we necessarily now have less of. You know... tires, radios, gas, fuel, food, fun, leisure and all the like. In its own way, your bottle of ice-cold Coca-Cola, or your glass of Coke at the soda fountain, is almost a casual symbol of such pleasant things.

"Everybody eagerly accepts wartime restrictions.

We'll have the good things, again, someday. But now it's work harder and fight, too. We've got a tough war to win. And no matter what anybody is doing to help (this doesn't go for fighting men) nobody is doing his full share if he's not buying U. S. War Bonds and War Stamps regularly. Are *you* buying them? Are you buying your share in Victory and in the good American way of life?"

War Bonds were a popular and patriotic method of raising money to finance the immense war effort. Hollywood movie stars and famous radio personalities made bond tours along with returning war heroes, raising millions of dollars for the government. In this instance Sprite, who had not yet totally disappeared from Coca-Cola's advertising, proclaims the necessity of "buying your share in Victory and in the good American way of life". (1943)

That _Extra_ Something!

...You can spot it every time

1863 "Stonewall Jackson taught us what _the pause that refreshes_ really means."

A new idea joined the army in "the sixties". It was the rest pause ... with refreshment. Here's what a Coca-Cola advertisement said about it in 1931:—

"Stonewall Jackson always got there first. On the march he gave his men rations of sugar and at intervals required them to lie down for a short rest. Thus he marched troops farther and faster than any other general in the field. Since his day all marching troops have been given a short rest period out of every hour."

To our fighting men and war workers everywhere that fact has new importance. A short pause helps you in any task. A pause for the energy-giving refreshment of ice-cold Coca-Cola helps you even more.

1918 Back in 1918 our fighting men thrilled to certain things. One was, "The mail's in". Another was, "It's pay day". A big one was, "Ice-cold Coca-Cola".

1943 Today _the pause that refreshes_ with ice-cold Coca-Cola is a standby of men in the Army, Navy and Marine Corps—and a standby of the great army of men and women war workers. Every time you enjoy a Coke it tells you all over again what it means to morale.

Even with war and so many Coca-Cola bottling plants in enemy-occupied countries our fighting men are delighted to find Coca-Cola being bottled in so many places all over the globe.

Coca-Cola 5¢

The best is always the better buy!

COPYRIGHT 1943, THE COCA-COLA COMPANY

Confederate General "Stonewall" Jackson was an authentic national hero to millions of Americans. In this advertisement Coca-Cola recycled a 1931 company ad that praised Jackson's concern for his troops on the march, which included a sugar ration and brief hourly rest periods. Coke apparently viewed _The Pause That Refreshes_ as the natural inheritor of this Civil War procedure during WWII. (1943)

"Caps off to our fighting men"

MINIMUM CONTENTS
6 FLUID OZS.

Coca-Cola

REG. U.S. PAT. OFF.

"Next to wives, sweethearts and letters from home, among things our soldiers mention most is Coca-Cola. Of course, our fighting men meet up with Coke many places overseas. But Coca-Cola got there first. Yes siree, Coca-Cola has been a globe-trotter since way back when. It has been sold in more than 100 foreign lands. Even with war and so many Coca-Cola bottling plants in enemy-occupied countries, our fighting men are delighted to find Coca-Cola being bottled right on the spot in so many places around the globe. And do they go for it when they find it! Who doesn't?"

• • •

Did you know this? There are Coca-Cola bottling plants in: Australia, England, New Zealand, South Africa, Canada, India, Iceland, Spain, Bermuda, Cuba, Mexico, Jamaica, Trinidad, Newfoundland, Haiti, Dominican Republic, Nassau, Argentina, Bolivia, Brazil, British Guiana, Chile, Colombia, Dutch Guiana, Ecuador, Peru, Uruguay, Venezuela, British Honduras, Costa Rica, Guatemala, Honduras, Nicaragua, Panama, El Salvador.

COPYRIGHT 1943, THE COCA-COLA COMPANY

Sprite made his last appearance in Coke's wartime advertising with this June 1943 message about the company's worldwide bottling facilities. While Coca-Cola was not available in Germany during the war, the company's plants continued to produce a substitute known as Fanta, and empty Coke bottles were used to stockpile water for civilian use when Allied air raids cut off the regular water supply. (1943)

That Extra Something!

...You can spot it every time

Word comes back again and again from those who have been at far-flung fronts that next to wives, sweethearts and letters from home among the things our fighting men mention most is Coca-Cola . . . Coke.

Is it hard to realize how this famous soft drink could mean so much to so many? Remembrance of its taste and refreshment sailed with them. Ice-cold Coca-Cola was their associate on bright, happy occasions. Part of their growing up . . . a pleasant thing to remember and look forward to. A reminder of home ways.

Even so far away from home, each time they enjoy it, they realize that the only thing like Coca-Cola is Coca-Cola, itself.

Although war has changed and disrupted so many things in their lives, our fighting forces overseas are so often delighted to find in far-off places an old familiar friend . . . Coca-Cola . . . being bottled in Allied Nations all over the globe, just as it is at home.

When you write to the boys in Service, try to limit your letters only to those close to you by family or friendship. Remember, Uncle Sam wants the boys to hear from home, but preferably from those nearest and dearest to them.

Few things equal the thrill of knowing that someone they know and love is caring, is thinking, is writing.

Drink **Coca-Cola** TRADE-MARK

Delicious and Refreshing

The best is always the better buy!

5¢

COPYRIGHT 1943, THE COCA-COLA COMPANY

Most US Marines would be very surprised to find their smiling sergeant delivering the company's mail as depicted in this September 1943 Coca-Cola advertisement. Marine victories in the Pacific theatre were well publicized, and the Army and the Navy often complained that the Marines received an inordinate amount of publicity and advertising opportunities due to the Corps' excessive public relations efforts. However, the Marines also suffered the highest percentage of casualties. (1943)

The rest-pause that refreshes

Welcome in peace... more welcome in war work

MANAGERS and personnel directors will tell you that regular rest-pauses plus the refreshment of ice-cold Coca-Cola increase contentment in their plants. Thus production is increased. A pause for Coca-Cola is a little thing in itself, but it's one of those little things that brightens a busy day.

You might think it strange that workers have such a welcome for a 5¢ soft drink. But Coca-Cola has something all its own in goodness. Made with a finished art, it has taste that always pleases. And more than just quenching thirst, it brings a happy after-sense of complete refreshment. The only thing like Coca-Cola is Coca-Cola, itself.

Letters from plant managers from coast to coast emphasize that the little moment for an ice-cold Coca-Cola means a lot to workers in war plants. It's a refreshing moment on the sunny side of things . . . a way to turn to refreshment without turning from work.

Hard work, rush work, hot work. Wouldn't you, yourself, welcome a frosty bottle of Coca-Cola when it came your time to pause? Who wouldn't.

A breathing spell, a rest-pause and ice-cold Coca-Cola. Contentment comes when you connect with a Coke.

Drink

Coca-Cola
TRADE-MARK

Delicious and Refreshing

The best 5¢ is always the better buy!

COPYRIGHT 1943, THE COCA-COLA COMPANY

Men of military age working in vital industries were not allowed to enlist in the armed services, and were automatically deferred by their draft boards. Although women picked up a huge share of the civilian work load, there were some jobs that required the mens' physical strength or long term experience, and those workers labored long, hard hours to achieve production goals. This ad picks up again the theme of *rest-pause* that was featured in the earlier "Stonewall" Jackson advertisement. (1943)

That Extra Something!

...You can spot it every time

When war correspondents say that Coca-Cola is the drink of our fighting men, you know there is a reason for it. What drink offers such delicious taste and downright refreshment?

One tells how a Ranger, returned from Dieppe, asked for Coca-Cola in preference to anything. Another cables that the main event of the week for the doughboys at a desolate South Pacific outpost was 12 bottles of Coke. We read such things in the papers regularly.

Coca-Cola had to be good to earn fast friendship like that with our Armed Forces. Coca-Cola is good. It's made that way with a finished art and choicest ingredients. And with a taste all its own. Truly, the only thing like Coca-Cola is Coca-Cola, itself.

Although war has changed and disrupted so many things in their lives, our fighting forces overseas are so often delighted to find in far-off places an old familiar friend ... Coca-Cola ... being bottled in Allied Nations all over the globe, just as it is at home.

Wherever there's action in this world-wide war, you find the famous jeep. Wherever it's possible to get it, you'll find Coca-Cola, too, bringing refreshment to our fighting troops.

CANTEEN

You could see this going on many places in the world. When our soldiers get a chance to enjoy a pause, they make it *the pause that refreshes* with ice-cold Coca-Cola.

Drink
Coca-Cola
TRADE-MARK
Delicious and Refreshing

The best 5¢ is always the better buy!

COPYRIGHT 1943, THE COCA-COLA COMPANY

Essentially a Canadian operation, the Dieppe Raid of August 1942 mentioned in this advertising copy was a debacle, but wartime censorship kept that information from the Allied civilian population. When this ad appeared in August 1943 American men and women were stationed all over the world, and actually in combat in several areas. In preparation for the company's next major promotional campaign, Coca-Cola's copy referred regularly to its worldwide bottling efforts. (1943)

Have a "Coke" = Welcome, Friends

"Have A Coke" kicked off Coca-Cola's theme of universality that dominated the company's advertising for the duration of the war years. The campaign also incorporated *the global high-sign* into Coke's famous red logo. In mid-1943 American and Canadian troops had regained control of Attu and Kiska in the Aleutians, both occupied by the Japanese in June 1942. Alaska was an important stepping stone for transporting Lend-Lease supplies, including thousands of aircraft, to the Soviet Union. (1943)

...or how to get along in Alaska

The American soldier in Alaska meets up with many things that remind him of home. One of them is Coca-Cola. *Have a "Coke"* says he to a stranger, and in one simple gesture he has made a friend. In three words he has said, "You and I understand each other". *The pause that refreshes* works as well in the Yukon as it does in Youngstown. From Atlanta to the Seven Seas, Coca-Cola has become the high-sign between kindly-minded strangers, the symbol of a friendly way of living.

* * *

Next to mothers, wives, sweethearts and letters from home, one thing our soldiers overseas mention most is Coca-Cola. So you'll be delighted to know they frequently find it — bottled on the spot — in over 35 Allied and neutral nations 'round the globe.

"Coke" = Coca-Cola

It's natural for popular names to acquire friendly abbreviations. That's why you hear Coca-Cola called "Coke".

COPYRIGHT 1943, THE COCA-COLA COMPANY

Have a "Coke" = Good winds have blown you here

. . . *a way to say "We are friends" to the Chinese*

In far-off places, when Coca-Cola is on hand, you find it cementing friendships for our fighting men. China knew Coca-Cola from Tientsin to Shanghai, from Hong Kong to Tsingtao. To Chinese and Yank alike, *Have a "Coke"* are welcome words. They belong with friendliness and freedom. From Atlanta to the Seven Seas, Coca-Cola stands for *the pause that refreshes*—has become a symbol of good will among the friendly-minded.

* * *

Our fighting men are delighted to meet up with Coca-Cola many places overseas. Coca-Cola has been a globe-trotter "since way back when". Even with war, Coca-Cola today is being bottled right on the spot in over 35 allied and neutral nations.

"Coke" = Coca-Cola
It's natural for popular names to acquire friendly abbreviations. That's why you hear Coca-Cola called "Coke".

-the global high-sign

COPYRIGHT 1943, THE COCA-COLA COMPANY

American volunteer pilots known as the "Flying Tigers" were organized with tacit US government approval prior to Pearl Harbor to aid the Chinese in their war with Japan. Each fighter aircraft had a shark mouth painted on the nose, creating a ferocious appearance. Although not involved in combat until late December 1941, in only six months of operations their exploits became legendary. Coke Continues its universality motif by saying "We are friends" to the Chinese. (1943)

After the successful invasion of North Africa in November 1942, the sector became the major staging area for operations in the Mediterranean region. The war was beginning to go well for the Allies by Christmas in 1943, and Americans had reasons to smile. General Eisenhower considered Coke so indispensable to the war effort that in June 1943 he had directed "ten separate machines [plants] for installation in different localities, each complete for bottling twenty thousand bottles per day". North Africa was one of the first. (1943)

Have a Coca-Cola = Merry Christmas

...or how Americans spread the holiday spirit overseas

Your American fighting man loves his lighter moments. Quick to smile, quick to enter the fun, he takes his home ways with him where he goes ... makes friends easily. *Have a "Coke"*, he says to stranger or friend, and he spreads the spirit of good will throughout the year. And throughout the world Coca-Cola stands for *the pause that refreshes*, —has become the high-sign of the friendly-hearted.

* * *

Our fighting men are delighted to meet up with Coca-Cola many places overseas. Coca-Cola has been a globe-trotter "since way back when". Even with war, Coca-Cola today is being bottled right on the spot in over 35 allied and neutral nations.

It's natural for popular names to acquire friendly abbreviations. That's why you hear Coca-Cola called "Coke".

Coca-Cola
-the global
high-sign

Have a "Coke" = Céad Míle Fáilte
(A HUNDRED THOUSAND WELCOMES)

...or how Americans make friends in Ireland

Céad Míle Fáilte—a hundred thousand welcomes —says the kindly Irishman when he meets a stranger. And it's got the same heart-warming friendliness as an Irish *Top o' the morning.* The American soldier says it another way. *Have a "Coke",* says he, and in three words he has said *Greetings, pal.* It's a phrase that works as well in Belfast as in Boston. Around the globe Coca-Cola stands for *the pause that refreshes,* —has become the high-sign between friendly-minded people.

* * *

Since 1886 Coca-Cola has spread around the world. Its refreshing goodness is welcomed by people around the globe. Despite the fact that many bottling plants are cut off in enemy-occupied lands, Coca-Cola is still being bottled in over 35 allied and neutral nations. So our fighting men can still enjoy it many places overseas.

"Coke" = Coca-Cola
It's natural for popular names to acquire friendly abbreviations. That's why you hear Coca-Cola called "Coke".

-the global high-sign

COPYRIGHT 1943, THE COCA-COLA COMPANY

Coca-Cola continued its universality advertising theme in 1944. While Ireland was not a belligerent during WWII, Northern Ireland, as part of the United Kingdom, most definitely was involved. Although this scene stresses relaxation in a bucolic rural setting, in the distance an American soldier can be seen walking a sentry post along a beach. More than 300,000 American servicemen and women served in Northern Ireland from 1942 to 1945, supporting FDR's promise to Winston Churchill that the US would defend this integral component of the UK. Note the American prefab Quonset huts across the lane from the thatched roof Irish cottage. (1944)

Have a Coca-Cola = As you were

...a way to relax on a battleship

Wherever a U. S. battleship may be, the American way of life goes along ... in sports, humor, customs and refreshment. So, naturally, Coca-Cola is there, too, met with frequently at the ship's soda fountain. *Have a "Coke"* is a phrase as common aboard a battle-wagon as it is ashore. It's a signal that spells out *We're pals.* From Atlanta to the Seven Seas, Coca-Cola stands for *the pause that refreshes, —* has become the symbol of happy comradeship.

* * *

Since 1886 Coca-Cola has spread around the world. Its refreshing goodness is welcomed by people around the globe. Despite the fact that many bottling plants are cut off in enemy-occupied lands, Coca-Cola is still being bottled in over 35 allied and neutral nations. So our fighting men can still enjoy it many places overseas.

It's natural for popular names to acquire friendly abbreviations. That's why you hear Coca-Cola called "Coke".

-the global high-sign

Life aboard a US battleship (2,300 men) or an aircraft carrier (3,500 men), differed from that experienced by the majority of wartime sailors on smaller ships. Most "Ship's Stores" available on US naval vessels during WWII were not as elaborate as the soda fountain in this illustration (which the sailors called a "geedunk stand"), but in the war zones the Navy did have superior facilities to the Army, mainly due to the ships' refrigeration systems. An ice-cold Coke, especially in the heat of the Pacific or other tropical duty stations, was only available in dreams to most ground combat troops. (1944)

New Zealand was an important staging area for the American forces in the Pacific Theater of Operations during WWII. The visiting Yanks got along extremely well (many marriages) with the local population, but it is doubtful that they mixed very often with the native Maori tribesmen. Interestingly, during the First World War soldiers of the British Empire, which included New Zealand, enjoyed a "lemon squash" called Kia Ora. Twenty-five years later that native expression is featured in this Coke ad. (1944)

Have a "Coke" = Kia Ora
(GOOD LUCK)

...or sealing friendships in New Zealand

Kia ora, says the New Zealander when he wants to give you his best wishes. It's a down-under way of telling you that you're a pal and that your welfare is a matter of mutual interest. The American soldier says it another way. *Have a "Coke",* says he, and in three words he has made a friend. It's a custom that has followed the flag from the tropics to the polar regions. It's a phrase that says *Welcome, neighbor* from Auckland to Albuquerque, from New Zealand to New Mexico. 'Round the globe, Coca-Cola stands for *the pause that refreshes,* —has become the high-sign between friendly-minded people.

*   *   *

In news stories, books and magazines, you read how much our fighting men cherish Coca-Cola whenever they get it. Yes, more than just a delicious and refreshing drink, "Coke" reminds them of happy times at home. Luckily, they find Coca-Cola —bottled on the spot—in over 35 allied and neutral countries 'round the globe.

Coca-Cola
-the global high-sign

"Coke" = Coca-Cola
It's natural for popular names to acquire friendly abbreviations. That's why you hear Coca-Cola called "Coke".

COPYRIGHT 1944, THE COCA-COLA COMPANY

Have a Coca-Cola = ¿Qué Hay, Amigo?

(WHAT GIVES, PAL?)

...or making pals in Panama

Down Panama way, American ideas of friendliness and good neighborliness are nothing new. Folks there understand and like our love of sports, our humor and our everyday customs. *Have a "Coke"*, says the American soldier, and the natives know he is saying *We are friends* ... the same friendly invitation as when you offer Coca-Cola from your own refrigerator at home. Everywhere Coca-Cola stands for *the pause that refreshes,*—has become the high-sign of kindly-minded people the world over.

*   *   *

In news stories, books and magazines, you read how much our fighting men cherish Coca-Cola whenever they get it. Yes, more than just a delicious and refreshing drink, "Coke" reminds them of happy times at home. Luckily, they find Coca-Cola —bottled on the spot—in over 35 allied and neutral countries 'round the globe.

Coca-Cola
REG. U.S. PAT. OFF.
·the global high-sign

It's natural for popular names to acquire friendly abbreviations. That's why you hear Coca-Cola called "Coke".

The Panama Canal is of great strategic and tactical value to the United States during any war, as it allows for the quick transfer of ships between the Atlantic and Pacific Oceans, negating the need for a long sea journey around Cape Horn at the southern tip of South America. During the Second World War the fear of enemy attack was always present, so the Canal remained well-defended by American forces for the duration. In this advertisement it appears that the well-fed Panamanian is bartering live chickens to the American soldiers, possibly for some of that Coca-Cola being unloaded from the *Panama Hattie* in the background! (1944)

Have a "Coke" = Ahoy, mates

United States' shipyards built 2,770 Liberty cargo ships from 1941-45, as well as thousands of warships for the Navy. Without cargo ships to transport America's enormous defense production it would have been difficult, if not impossible, to defeat the Axis powers simultaneously all over the globe. The woman in the yellow sweater featured in this advertisement is apparently an inspector, while the woman to her right is a welder. Men working in the shipyards were deferred from military service due to the vital nature of their occupation. (1944)

...or keeping up the good work

Faster and faster the ships go down the ways in the wartime ship-building program. From sunny California to the coast of Maine, workers have learned that *the pause that refreshes* helps everybody do *more* work and *better* work. *Have a "Coke"* says a hard-working shipbuilder to his mates. It's a little minute long enough for a big rest. Whether in a shipyard or in your own living room, Coca-Cola stands for *the pause that refreshes,*—has become a symbol of friendly relaxation.

* * *

Our fighting men meet up with Coca-Cola many places overseas, where it's bottled on the spot. Coca-Cola has been a globe-trotter "since way back when".

Coca-Cola
-the global high-sign

"Coke" = Coca-Cola
It's natural for popular names to acquire friendly abbreviations. That's why you hear Coca-Cola called "Coke".

Have a "Coke" = Pukka Gen
(SWELL INFO.)

...or how friends are made in the R. A. F.

Have a "Coke" is a friendly greeting among R.A.F. flyers back at early dawn from a night mission. It's a salute among comrades in arms that seals the bonds of friendship in Plymouth, England, as in Plymouth, Mass. It's an offer as welcome on an English airfield as it is in your own living room. Around the globe, Coca-Cola stands for *the pause that refreshes,*—has become a happy symbol of good-hearted friendliness.

*   *   *

Our fighting men are delighted to meet up with Coca-Cola many places overseas. Coca-Cola has been a globe-trotter "since way back when". Even with war, Coca-Cola today is being bottled right on the spot in over 35 allied and neutral nations.

-the global high-sign

"Coke" = Coca-Cola

It's natural for popular names to acquire friendly abbreviations. That's why you hear Coca-Cola called "Coke".

COPYRIGHT 1944 THE COCA-COLA COMPANY

"Pukka Gen" was a military slang term for credible information popular with British servicemen who had seen service in India. The RAF Bomber Command flew its missions over Europe at night and suffered 55% casualties from enemy fighters and antiaircraft fire. The damage to this bomber is very visible on the aircraft fuselage behind this air crew. The painted bullseye is an RAF roundel, symbol of British military aviation. The Brits enjoyed a Coke whenever they could get one! (1944)

Have a Coca-Cola = Howdy, Neighbor

...or greeting friends at home and abroad

One of the first places they head for, when they get back, is the neighborhood soda fountain and all its old associations...among them, Coca-Cola. Many places overseas, too, your American fighting man meets up with that old friend...ice-cold Coca-Cola. It's always like word from home to hear the friendly greeting *Have a "Coke"* in a strange land.

Yes, around the globe, Coca-Cola stands for *the pause that refreshes,*—has become a symbol of our way of living.

* * *

In news stories, books and magazines, you read how much our fighting men cherish Coca-Cola whenever they get it. Luckily, they find Coca-Cola available in over 35 allied and neutral countries 'round the globe.

-the global high-sign

It's natural for popular names to acquire friendly abbreviations. That's why you hear Coca-Cola called "Coke".

The drug store lunch counter was a fixture of American community life during the 1940s, a place where townspeople of all ages gathered to talk about the activities of the day while enjoying a sandwich and a Coke. The appearance of a local man returned safely from the war, in this case an Army pilot wearing captain's bars on his shoulder, certainly captures the attention of this youngster and his sister and mother. Unfortunately, it is not possible from the artist's angle to determine whether the soda fountain attendant's eyes are focused on the aerial maneuver being illustrated or the pretty blond young lady observing the demonstration! (1944)

Have a "Coke" = How are things goin'?

...or being friendly in Newfoundland

There's an American way to make new-found friends in Newfoundland. It's the cheery invitation *Have a "Coke"*—an old U. S. custom that is reaching 'round the world. It says *Let's be friends*—reminds Yanks of home. In many lands around the globe, Coca-Cola stands for *the pause that refreshes,*—has become a symbol of our friendly home-ways. So Coca-Cola belongs in your home, too...ice-cold and ready in the refrigerator. Get a supply today.

* * *

Our fighting men meet up with Coca-Cola many places overseas. Coca-Cola has been a globe-trotter "since way back when". Even with war, Coca-Cola today is being bottled right on the spot in over 35 allied and neutral nations.

-the global high-sign

"Coke" = Coca-Cola
It's natural for popular names to acquire friendly abbreviations. That's why you hear Coca-Cola called "Coke".

In May 1941, two weeks after The Lend-Lease Act was signed into law by President Roosevelt, the United States took over the British Naval Base at Argentia, Newfoundland. It became an important stepping stone in crossing the Atlantic for both American aircraft and ship convoys on their way to the United Kingdom. While the people were hospitable to the American servicemen stationed in their country, the local weather most certainly was not. It may have been conducive to catching codfish, but the cold and fog made the situation difficult for the troops on duty. A Coke and a smile made life more bearable for both civilians and military personnel. (1944)

The American military was racially segregated during WWII and black Americans were rarely portrayed in any advertisements that were not targeted to black publications and audiences. However, black military personnel played increasingly important roles as the war progressed, and Coca-Cola was willing to break down some of those barriers with this August 1944 advertisement featuring a black soldier from an engineering unit enjoying a Coke—and his birthright. (1944)

Have a "Coke" = Soldier, refresh yourself

...or a way to relax in camp

From southern camps with their moss-hung cypresses to camps near the north woods, there's one place soldiers can relax—the Post Exchange. There they settle down to "shoot the breeze" together. *Have a "Coke"*, they say. Coca-Cola is a refreshing reminder of what they left behind. On "Company Street" in camp as on Main Street at home, Coca-Cola stands for *the pause that refreshes*. In your own refrigerator, ice-cold bottles of Coca-Cola are a symbol of a friendly way of living.

*   *   *

Our fighting men meet up with Coca-Cola many places overseas. Coca-Cola has become a globe-trotter "since way back when". Even with war, Coca-Cola today is bottled right on the spot in over 35 allied and neutral nations.

-the global high-sign

"Coke" = Coca-Cola
It's natural for popular names to acquire friendly abbreviations. That's why you hear Coca-Cola called "Coke".

COPYRIGHT 1944, THE COCA-COLA COMPANY

Have a Coca-Cola = You're my kind

...or allies enjoy a friendly pause

There's a friendly phrase that speaks the allied language. It's *Have a "Coke"*. Friendliness enters the picture when ice-cold Coca-Cola appears. Over tinkling glasses of ice-cold "Coke", minds meet and hearts are closer together. It's a happy custom that's spreading 'round the globe. Coca-Cola stands for *the pause that refreshes*, — has become an everyday high-sign of friendliness among people of good will.

* * *

Our fighting men meet up with Coca-Cola many places overseas, where it's bottled on the spot. Coca-Cola has been a globe-trotter "since way back when".

-the global high-sign

It's natural for popular names to acquire friendly abbreviations. That's why you hear Coca-Cola called "Coke".

While enjoying a five cent Coke, a Navy WAVE and a Marine Sergeant (all Marines were Marines, regardless of gender) wistfully contemplate the photograph of a "swabbie" who hopefully will be coming home to one of them, most likely the WAVE. The male "soda-jerk" behind the fountain has been replaced by a woman due to wartime demands on the available young men who normally filled this position. (1944)

Have a Coca-Cola = Refreshment calling

...the soda fountain shows the way

All over America, depots are crowded with soldiers, sailors and war workers busy getting a big job done. Across the land, cheerful soda fountains invite you to pause and go your way refreshed with ice-cold Coca-Cola. At home and abroad, Coca-Cola is the high-sign of friendly refreshment for people on the go.

* * *

Our fighting men meet up with Coca-Cola many places overseas, where it's bottled on the spot. Coca-Cola has been a globe-trotter "since way back when".

-the global high-sign

It's natural for popular names to acquire friendly abbreviations. That's why you hear Coca-Cola called "Coke".

COPYRIGHT 1944, THE COCA-COLA COMPANY

Railroads were the primary mode of transportation on the domestic front during WWII, and the stations were filled to capacity from early morning until late at night. Sleeping soldiers and sailors hung signs on themselves indicating what time they needed to awaken in order to make a train connection, and station personnel invariably complied with their requests. Military police were usually present, randomly checking orders to catch any service-men who had "hopped the fence" and to control inappropriate behavior. Their services were rarely needed, as most of the young men far from home just want to grab some sleep, which they learned to do anywhere, anytime. It would have been highly unusual for the soldier saying goodbye to his wife and child in this ad to be carrying a rifle in an American railroad station, to say the least. However, enjoying a Coca-Cola helped pass the time. (1944)

Greetings, brother . . . Have a Coca-Cola

. . . or initiating a new subject of Neptune

It's a fine old custom—the good-natured initiation of those who cross the equator for the first time. In much the same spirit of good-natured fun, people everywhere respond to the fine old invitation *Have a "Coke"*. That's when friendliness speaks a refreshing language all its own. A pause for ice-cold Coca-Cola is always greeted with a smile in so many places, on the seas and overseas, just as it is in your home.

It's a happy symbol among people who understand the pleasant ways of friendship.

* * *

Our fighting men meet up with Coca-Cola many places overseas, where it's bottled on the spot. Coca-Cola has been a globe-trotter "since way back when".

It's natural for popular names to acquire friendly abbreviations. That's why you hear Coca-Cola called "Coke".

Crossing the Equator has been a special occasion for seafaring men for hundreds of years. All the "polywogs", or first-timers, had to be initiated by the "shellbacks", and rank held no privileges at all. The brooms in the hands of the "shellbacks" were used to swat the backsides of "polywogs" as they crawled through part of the initiation. The sprinkling of Marines in this illustration suggests that the ship is a transport carrying these men to one of the savage battles the Marines fought in the island hopping campaign that defined the Pacific War. King Neptune, usually a Navy Chief Petty Officer with about 20 years service, holds court on this American ship. The three-pronged spear known as a trident was his symbol of authority. (1944)

Esta p'ra mim ... Have a Coke
(THIS IS FOR ME)

...or how to be buddies in Brazil

Down Rio way, sun-soaked Copacabana Beach lures folks from everywhere to enjoy fun and relaxation. Many a visitor meets an old friend there—in Coca-Cola. Your American sailor on shore leave knows that the invitation *Have a Coke* is the sure-fire formula for how-to-make-friends. Those three words speak the language of friendliness straight from the heart. They say *I like the cut of your jib—let's get to know each*

other better. Whether in Rio or in Richmond, when you say *Have a Coke* you've said it all, in a way that people like and understand. *The pause that refreshes* with ice-cold Coca-Cola is a happy symbol of friendliness everywhere.

* * *

Our fighting men meet up with Coca-Cola many places overseas, where it's bottled on the spot. Coca-Cola has been a globe-trotter "since way back when".

-the global high-sign

"Coke" = Coca-Cola
You naturally hear Coca-Cola called by its friendly abbreviation "Coke". Both mean the quality product of The Coca-Cola Company.

COPYRIGHT 1945, THE COCA-COLA COMPANY

While Brazil has very little recognition as a fighting ally during WWII, its physical location was of immense importance to the US Army Air Forces. American bomber aircraft destined for the European theater and flying the "southern route" departed Brazil across the South Atlantic for their destinations in North Africa and Italy. It was not an easy flight. The permanent military garrisons in Brazil had the opportunity to play as hard as they worked, as evidenced by this illustration of life on one of Brazil's famous beaches. A Coca-Cola usually sufficed for an introduction to the fair sex. (1944)

Christmas at home with the family was the dream for most American servicemen in 1944, and as the war apparently neared its conclusion, at least in Europe, it was a reality for a few American boys. While their Army uniforms do not display their specific branches of service, these four young men are enjoying the holiday at the home of one of them. Electric trains, chocolates, a fishing rod, a viewmaster and their boys safe at home made a complete Christmas for some lucky families in 1944. And Coca-Cola only made it that much better. (1944)

Have a "Coke" = Merry Christmas

...*adding refreshment to holiday cheer*

The spirit of good will rules the Christmas season. It's a time to get together with friends and family . . . a time when all we mean by *home* in its graciousness and friendliness is at its peak. In such an atmosphere Coca-Cola belongs, ice-cold and sparkling with life. There's a whole story of hospitality in the three words *Have a "Coke"*,—three words that express a friendly spirit the whole year 'round. Yes, Coca-Cola and *the pause that refreshes* are everyday symbols of a way of living that takes friendliness for granted.

* * *

Our fighting men meet up with Coca-Cola many places overseas, where it's bottled on the spot. Coca-Cola has been a globe-trotter "since way back when".

-the global high-sign

"Coke" = Coca-Cola
It's natural for popular names to acquire friendly abbreviation. That's why you hear Coca-Cola called "Coke".

'Eia ke ola...Have a Coke
(HERE'S HEALTH)

The beautiful Hawaiian Islands were a strange mixture of an idyllic polynesian society and determined military activity in early 1945. The Islands were still a central staging area for the Pacific war, although the fighting had shifted thousands of miles westward as American forces closed in on Japan. The native girl displays a flower behind her right ear, indicating she is socially unattached. This is apparently agreeable to all three of the young men surrounding her, and Coca-Cola adds to the convivial gathering. (1945)

...or winning a welcome in Wailuku

Here's health is the happy expression of Hawaiian hospitality. Just as friendly is the *Have a Coke* of the Army flyer. In these three words he says *We're pals.* On a Hawaiian beach, where fishermen toss their nets in the sea...just as in your own home...Coca-Cola brings friendly refreshment to all comers. In Wailuku or Wichita, Coca-Cola stands for *the pause that refreshes,*—has become a symbol of a friendly way of living. Keep Coke on hand in your refrigerator—for your family and your guests.

*   *   *

Our fighting men meet up with Coca-Cola many places overseas, where it's bottled on the spot. Coca-Cola has been a globe-trotter "since way back when".

Coke=Coca-Cola
It's natural for popular names to acquire friendly abbreviations. That's why you hear Coca-Cola called Coke.

COPYRIGHT 1945, THE COCA-COLA COMPANY

So glad to see you... Have a Coca-Cola

...or today's friendships help make the future

Down where springtime is on the way...and on up north from there ... sentimental is the word for them all. Miss America, G. I. Joe, Mom and Dad, you and the folks next door just naturally want to make friends. When you meet up with someone whom you are glad to see, try the greeting *Have a Coke*. When you invite people to share *the pause that refreshes* with ice-cold Coca-Cola, they know that you have your hand out and your heart open. Next time you meet, they will want to be the first to say *Have a Coke*.

*   *   *

Our fighting men meet up with Coca-Cola many places overseas, where it's bottled on the spot. Coca-Cola has been a globe-trotter "since way back when".

It's natural for popular names to acquire friendly abbreviations. That's why you hear Coca-Cola called Coke.

With the end of the war imminent in Europe and continued US successes in the Pacific, it became acceptable for young men of military age, as illustrated by the background personalities in this ad, to been seen out of uniform in public without being labeled as "draft-dodgers". However, a returning swabbie still holds the attention of two attractive members of the fair sex at the town ice cream parlor, where their legs as well as Coca-Cola are prominently displayed. (1945)

La moda Americana ... Have a Coke
(THE AMERICAN WAY)

... or an American custom as seen in Italy

One of the interesting things that impresses people overseas about the American fighting man is his friendliness among his fellows. Everywhere they see Americans bringing with them their customs and home-ways—their own brand of open-heartedness. *Have a Coke*, foreigners hear the G. I. say when he wants to be friendly, and they begin to understand what America means. For in this simple gesture is some of the essence of Main Street and the family fireside. Yes, the custom of *the pause that refreshes* with ice-cold Coca-Cola helps show the world the friendliness of American ways.

*   *   *

Our fighting men meet up with Coca-Cola many places overseas, where it's bottled on the spot. Coca-Cola has been a globe-trotter "since way back when".

-the global high-sign

"Coke" = Coca-Cola
You naturally hear Coca-Cola called by its friendly abbreviation "Coke". Both mean the quality product of The Coca-Cola Company.

The friendliness displayed by American soldiers towards local populations, especially children, was legendary during WWII. "Have a Coke" often initiated the camaraderie between the military and local civilians. Italy signed an armistice with the Allies in 1943, but the German Army continued to fight tenaciously and remained in Italy until the end of the war. The presence of naval officers ashore in this advertisement indicates that this scene is in a rear area, probably near a major port such as Naples. The infantrymen are wearing the blue and white shoulder patch of the Third Infantry Division, which fought in North Africa, Sicily, Italy, France and Germany. It was known as the "Rock of the Marne" for its service in WWI in France. (1945)

The local doctor and pharmacist benignly observe a proud father displaying this young soldier's military decorations at the drug store soda fountain. They include the Silver Star, Purple Heart and Good Conduct Medal. The soldier is certainly the star attraction to the two attentive young ladies seated next to him, and also to the female fountain attendant who is about to serve another Coca-Cola. (1945)

Just like old times...Have a Coca-Cola

...or meeting-up time at the fountain

Everybody meets everybody at the soda fountain. It's the neighborhood meeting place. That's where your G. I., home on furlough, can get back in touch with the local goings-on. That's where the words *Have a Coke* start new friendships and seal old ones. Yes, Coca-Cola, tingling with life and sparkle, is the center of attraction, inviting all comers to join up,

be refreshed and feel friendly. Drop in at the soda fountain today yourself and meet up with *the pause that refreshes* with ice-cold Coke. You'll like it...lots.

*   *   *

Our fighting men meet up with Coca-Cola many places overseas, where it's bottled on the spot. Coca-Cola has been a globe-trotter "since way back when".

Coca-Cola
-the global
high-sign

You naturally hear Coca-Cola called by its friendly abbreviation "Coke". Both mean the quality product of The Coca-Cola Company.

Da's na fijn, zunne!...Have a Coke
(SAY, THAT'S GREAT)

...a friendly American custom lands in Brussels

In Flemish, it's *vriendelijkheid*. In American, it's the plain, everyday word *friendliness*. And everywhere your Yankee doughboy goes, it comes spontaneously from his heart in a good old home-town phrase, *Have a Coke*. That's the way he's letting our democratic allies know why he does the friendly things he does. Friendliness is bred in his bone, and to kindred spirits it bubbles out — like the bubbling goodness of Coca-Cola itself and everything American that's behind it. Yes, *the pause that refreshes* with ice-cold Coke becomes an ambassador of good will ... a bit of the old home spirit carried across the seas.

* * *

Our fighting men meet up with Coca-Cola many places overseas, where it's bottled on the spot. Coca-Cola has been a globe-trotter "since way back when".

Coca-Cola

-the global high-sign

"Coke" = Coca-Cola
You naturally hear Coca-Cola called by its friendly abbreviation "Coke". Both mean the quality product of The Coca-Cola Company.

Brussels, Belgium's capital city, endured four years of occupation by German forces until it was liberated by the Allies in September 1944. Many residents had been forced to leave the city in search of food, and transportation was primitive, but the local population was overjoyed to be free. In this advertisement the attention of the American soldiers is centered on the rather engaging young woman who has just joined them for a Coke. The Belgian men will have to wait their turn. (1945)

Checkmate, pardner... Have a Coca-Cola

... refreshment fulfills a friendly mission

The location ... an airfield somewhere in the Pacific area. The place ... a recreation hut. The flyers ... veterans all. The drink ... Coca-Cola, served from its red dispenser just as at familiar soda fountains at home. Thus do fighting men get together for friendly recreation many places across the seas. The phrase *Have a Coke* expresses the friendliness and hospitality that come second-nature to your Yankee fighting man. It's his way of saying, *Pardner, you belong; you're a good Joe.* Wherever they meet up with Coca-Cola, they find in *the familiar pause that refreshes* a flashback to their own way of living —friendliness and refreshment all wrapped up in one happy, home-like moment.

* * *

Our fighting men meet up with Coca-Cola many places overseas, where it's bottled on the spot. Coca-Cola has been a globe-trotter "since way back when".

Coca-Cola
—the global high-sign

You naturally hear Coca-Cola called by its friendly abbreviation "Coke". Both mean the quality product of The Coca-Cola Company.

Throughout the spring of 1945 US B-29 bombing raids devastated Japan's cities. The American aviators involved paid a high price, as the Japanese governmzent declared them war criminals and executed many of them who were forced to parachute over enemy territory. When this advertisement was published in August 1945, Japan had just announced its acceptance of the Allied surrender terms. Thus the chess game could continue and Cokes could be enjoyed, for the war was over for these brave American Air Force air crews. (1945)

Get cracking, pal...Have a Coke
(DO YOUR STUFF)

...or it's fun to make friends

It's an international event that always comes off smoothly when fighting men of Canada, Britain and the U. S. A. get together for a bit of sociability. Especially when there's Coca-Cola around to add friendliness to new acquaintance. *Have a Coke* is an invitation that everybody understands, whether it's spoken with a Canadian, British or American accent —or any accent in the world. It means *I'm for*

you, chum; we can get along—from Los Angeles to London, from Macon to Montreal. At most any stop on the globe, *the pause that refreshes* with ice-cold Coca-Cola is a familiar symbol of good will.

* * *

Our fighting men meet up with Coca-Cola many places overseas, where it's bottled on the spot. Coca-Cola has been a globe-trotter "since way back when".

-the global high-sign

"Coke" = Coca-Cola
You naturally hear Coca-Cola called by its friendly abbreviation "Coke". Both mean the quality product of The Coca-Cola Company.

COPYRIGHT 1945, THE COCA-COLA COMPANY

National priorities and politics often interfere with alliances between countries, but during WWII the unity of the Allies was a major component of victory. Featured in this advertisement, which was actually published after the end of the war, are a Canadian sergeant, two US Navy enlisted men, an American technical sergeant and a British flying officer. As these assorted warriors sip their Cokes, they are playing a friendly game with aircraft identification flip cards, training devices used to assist in enemy versus friendly aircraft recognition. The poster on the wall features a man's head with his lips taped shut. The caption reads "Closed for the Duration—Loose Talk Can Cost Lives". (1945)

Une perm' a Paris...Have a Coca-Cola
(PARIS LEAVE)

...*Yank friendliness comes to the Eiffel Tower*

It's a natural impulse for a Yank soldier to share his home ways and home things with friendly foreigners abroad. The invitation *Have a Coke* is a symbol of his feeling of friendliness toward folks in Paris. It says *We're your allies—we wish you well* in a way as American as baseball or the corner drugstore at home. Wherever you hear *Have a Coke* you hear the voice of America...inviting you to enjoy *the pause that refreshes,—*a national custom now becoming an international symbol of good will as well.

* * *

Our fighting men meet up with Coca-Cola many places overseas, where it's bottled on the spot. Coca-Cola has been a globe-trotter "since way back when".

Coca-Cola
-the global high-sign

You naturally hear Coca-Cola called by its friendly abbreviation "Coke". Both mean the quality product of The Coca-Cola Company.

COPYRIGHT 1945, THE COCA-COLA COMPANY

The "City of Lights" had been darkened by four long years of German occupation until its liberation in August 1944. Hitler ordered the destruction of Paris but the local military commander ignored him and surrendered the city to the Allies. With the Eiffel Tower rising in the background, this American soldier appears to be trading a Coke for a bouquet of flowers, soon to be in the hands of a pretty Parisian girl. The age of the flower seller may indicate that she is wearing black for the loss of a loved one in the First World War. (1945)

US Navy Construction Battalions (CBs), known as Seabees, performed construction miracles throughout the war. In addition to their prodigious efforts in support of the military, these professional builders often assisted the local populace in reconstructing their shattered communities.

American personnel were exposed to many different cultures in the various war zones, as evidenced by this friendly confrontation between modern and primitive communications in the Admiralty Islands. The boys may be chatting, but they aren't giving away their Cokes. (1945)

Now you're talking...Have a Coca-Cola

...or tuning in refreshment on the Admiralty Isles

When battle-seasoned Seabees pile ashore in the Admiralty's, the world's longest refreshment counter is there to serve them at the P. X. Up they come tired and thirsty, and *Have a Coke* is the phrase that says *That's for me*—meaning friendly relaxation and refreshment. Coca-Cola is a bit of America that has travelled 'round the globe, catching up with our fighting men in so many far away places—reminding them of home—bringing them *the pause that refreshes*—the happy symbol of a friendly way of life.

*   *   *

Our fighting men meet up with Coca-Cola many places overseas, where it's bottled on the spot. Coca-Cola has been a globe-trotter "since way back when".

Coca-Cola
-the global
high-sign

You naturally hear Coca-Cola called by its friendly abbreviation "Coke". Both mean the quality product of The Coca-Cola Company.

Step right up, amigos...Have a Coke

...Yank friendliness comes back to Leyte

Naturally Filipinos thrilled when their Yankee comrades-in-arms came back to the Philippines. Freedom came back with them. Fair play took the place of fear. But also they brought back the old sense of friendliness that America stands for. You find it quickly expressed in the simple phrase *Have a Coke.* There's no easier or warmer way to say *Relax and be yourself.* Everywhere *the pause that refreshes* with ice-cold Coca-Cola has become a symbol of good will—an everyday example of how Yankee friendliness follows the flag around the globe.

* * *

Our fighting men meet up with Coca-Cola many places overseas, where it's bottled on the spot. Coca-Cola has been a globe-trotter "since way back when".

-the global high-sign

"Coke" = Coca-Cola
You naturally hear Coca-Cola called by its friendly abbreviation "Coke". Both mean the quality product of The Coca-Cola Company

COPYRIGHT 1945, THE COCA-COLA COMPANY

The Commonwealth of the Philippines was invaded in December 1941 and fell to the Japanese in the spring of 1942, but most of the population remained loyal to the United States throughout World War II. The Filipino people resisted the Japanese tenaciously and at a great cost in lives. General MacArthur's successful return in 1944-45 led initially to liberation and ultimately to independence for their country. In this ad two natives are offered Coca-Cola in GI canteen cups, dispensed by a khaki-colored Coke machine. (1945)

Christmas together... Have a Coca-Cola

At Christmas in 1945 Santa was replaced by an Army corporal and his gift sack was replaced by an Army knapsack, but Coca-Cola remains an unchanging ingredient of the holiday. The theme of a safe return to home and family was irresistible to most American advertisers, and rightly so. For the first Christmas in five years, Americans knew that their loved ones were secure and the killing was over, at least until the next war. (1945)

...*welcoming a fighting man home from the wars*

Time of all times. Home at last...to wife, to child and to family. With Christmas in the air and the tree lighted brightly. All the dreams of a lifetime rolled into one moment. A home-like, truly American moment where the old familiar phrase *Have a Coke* adds the final refreshing touch. Coca-Cola belongs to just such a time of friendly, warm family feeling. That's why you find it in homes big and small across the nation... the drink that adds life and sparkle to living. A happy moment is an occasion for Coke—and the happy American custom, *the pause that refreshes.*

*   *   *

Our fighting men meet up with Coca-Cola many places overseas, where it's bottled on the spot. Coca-Cola has been a globe-trotter "since way back when".

Coca-Cola
REG U S PAT OFF
-the global high-sign

"Coca-Cola" and its abbreviation "Coke" are the registered trademarks which distinguish the product of The Coca-Cola Company.

COPYRIGHT 1945, THE COCA-COLA COMPANY

Everybody's happy...Have a Coke

...*the pause that refreshes brightens the trip*

A familiar custom followed them when they went overseas...*the pause that refreshes* with ice-cold Coca-Cola. *Have a Coke* was a welcome greeting heard at one time or another behind nearly every fighting front. Now they are headed for home. Back to the folks, their friends, the old home town and the gang. Back to their American kind of life...with its happy ways and customs. In far away lands, ice-cold Coke brought them a touch of home, a glow of friendliness. It brought life, sparkle and comradeship to brighten many a drab moment...just as it goes on brightening happy moments at home.

Drink

Coca-Cola

REG. U.S. PAT. OFF.

Coke ☰ Coca-Cola
"Coca-Cola" and its abbreviation "Coke" are the registered trademarks which distinguish the product of The Coca-Cola Company.

COPYRIGHT 1945, THE COCA-COLA COMPANY

By early 1946 it was time for Coca-Cola to move on and leave wartime advertising behind. These happy young men and women representing several military services have apparently been demobilized and are heading home to resume their civilian lives that had been disrupted by the war. Millions of veterans attended college assisted by the GI Bill. Others who were not sure about their post-military careers joined the 52-20 Club—$20 dollars a week for 52 weeks provided by a grateful government. Wherever they went, Coca-Cola went with them, an integral part of their past and future lives. (1946)

ABOUT THE AUTHOR

V. DENNIS WRYNN was born in New York City just prior to World War II and retains vivid memories of civil defense blackouts, rationing, scrap drives and V-J Day. He is the author of two books about the homefront, *Detroit Goes to War*, which examines the automotive industry during the war years, and *Forge of Freedom*, a photo history of aircraft production in the U.S. during WWII. He currently leads tours to historical military sites around the world, writes extensively about military and aviation history and is an historical consultant to *Semper Fi* Video Productions in Stockton, California. Mr. Wrynn resides with his family in Fairfax Station, Virginia.